LEARN
TOGETHER

NUMBER WORK 3
Addition, subtraction, number bonds

Sandra Soper

A Piccolo Original
Piccolo Books

Note to parents

The aim of this book is to encourage your child to read and write at home. Young children love to copy. If you read and write with pleasure and purpose, your child will want to copy you. Also, the enthusiasm you show for the work in this book will rub off on the child. The activities are designed to be interesting and enjoyable: young children absorb more when they are happy and interested. Concentration varies from child to child, but 10 to 20 minutes per session is a good guide. Watch out for signs of weariness and stop before the work becomes boring.

In this series we use flicked letters from the very beginning to make it easier for the child to progress to fully joined-up writing. This has long been seen as good practice and is now recommended by the National Curriculum. Your child's school will have an agreed handwriting style. Find out what it is and use it whenever you write out something for the child to copy so that you complement the work of the school. It will hinder your child's progress if there is a conflict of advice between home and school.

Draw the tree minus the bird.	

Draw the snake minus its spots.	

Draw the boy minus his kite.	

Complete the number line then do the sums.

9   10   11   12

12 minus 3 = ☐   12 minus 7 = ☐

12 minus 1 = ☐   12 minus 4 = ☐

12 minus 2 = ☐   12 minus 11 = ☐

12 minus 0 = ☐   12 minus 5 = ☐

12 minus 10 = ☐   12 minus 12 = ☐

12 minus 8 = ☐   12 minus 9 = ☐

In each pair, circle the greater number.

4, 8	15, 10	12, 11
2, 1	19, 20	18, 14
3, 6	11, 17	16, 13

Write the answers in words.

Two more than one is

Ten more than five is

Eight more than six is

Seven more than two is

Nine more than one is

Write the number of grapes in each bunch in the boxes then add two more. Put down the new total in the circles. Write the sum about each picture underneath.

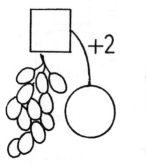 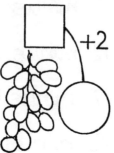 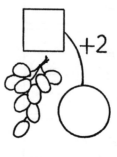 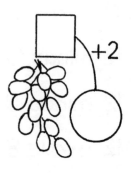

Draw a set of 4 fish. Colour 1 pink and 3 black. Now subset the fish into pink fish and black fish. Can you write a sum about this picture?

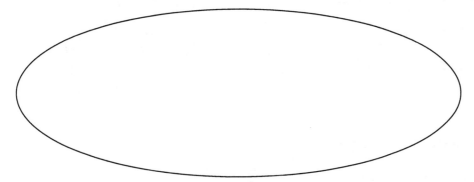

Do the same again but this time colour 2 fish black and 2 fish pink. What is the sum now?

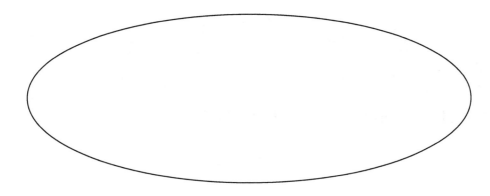

Finish these sums.

$4 = \square + 0$
$4 = 2 + \square$
$4 = \square + 1$
$4 = 0 + \square$
$4 = 3 + \square$
$4 = \square + 2$

Colour.

five 5

Count the skittles then cross them out to knock them down.

How many skittles? ▢

Knock down four. −4

How many now? ▢

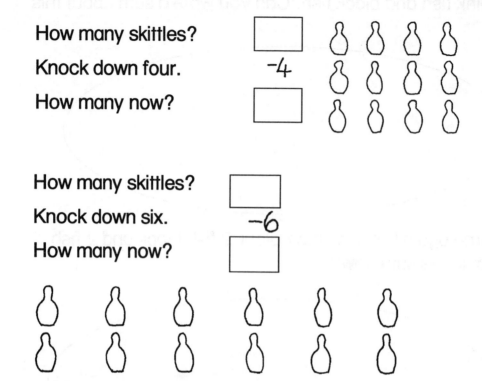

How many skittles? ▢

Knock down six. −6

How many now? ▢

Complete the number pairs to make 4.

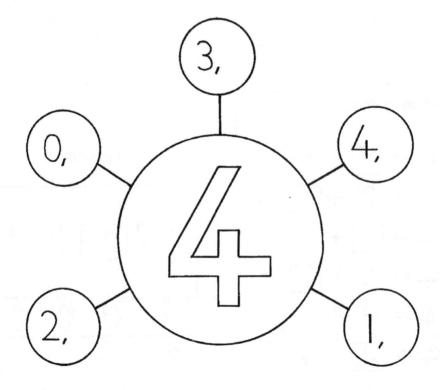

Count the total number of spots on each domino. Write this number in the top box. Cover the right half of each domino. How many spots now? Write this number in the bottom box. Read aloud the sum about this picture.

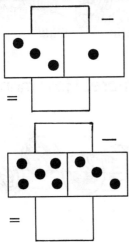

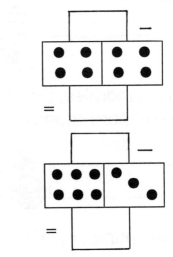

Write these sums in numbers.

Two take away two is nothing

Five take away three is two

Six take away one is five

Four take away one is three

Can you do these sums?

$$5 - 1 =$$
$$3 - 3 =$$
$$2 - 1 =$$
$$4 - 2 =$$
$$6 - 5 =$$

$$6 - 3 =$$
$$1 - 0 =$$
$$5 - 4 =$$
$$5 - 3 =$$
$$6 - 2 =$$

Mrs White baked thirteen cakes. She gave two to her friend. How many cakes were left?

| 13 |
| -2 |
| |

David had ten marbles, then he won three more. How many marbles were there altogether?

| 10 |
| +3 |
| |

Complete the number pairs.

3,   2,
1,   ③
    0,

0,   2,
   ② 1,

0,
   ①   1,

Draw a set of 2 apples and a set of 3 apples. Colour one apple green in each set. Subset the apples and write a sum about each set.

2 apples   3 apples

Sums. _____   _____

Draw 6 people at the bus stop.

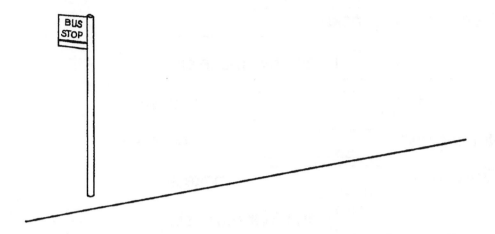

Complete the chain. Can you say it aloud with your eyes shut?

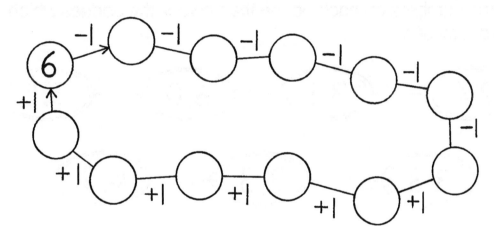

Can you do these sums?

☐ + 3 → 6   ☐ + 4 → 6

1 + ☐ → 6   0 + ☐ → 6

☐ + 1 → 6   3 + ☐ → 6

6 + ☐ → 6   4 + ☐ → 6

Fill in the missing words. Use cubes or rods to help, if you like.

Six and nothing make _____

_____ and two make six

Three and _____ make six

Nothing and _____ make six

Five and _____ make six

_____ and four make six

Add the numbers on each badge then colour the badges which have a total of 6.

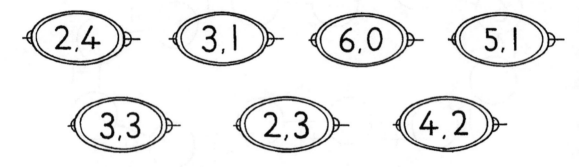

Write numbers on the second hill in the same order as those on the first hill.

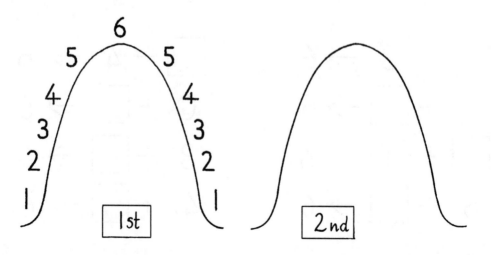

Draw 7 buttons then cross out 4.

How many buttons are left? [   ]

Copy the sum about this, then read it aloud.

seven	take	away	four	is	three

Now write the sum in numbers. [   ]

Can you do these sums?

7 take away 1 =   6 take away 0 =
4 take away 2 =   1 take away 1 =
3 take away 3 =   2 take away 1 =
5 take away 4 =   6 take away 3 =

Fill in the missing numbers and colour the beads, then read the pattern aloud.

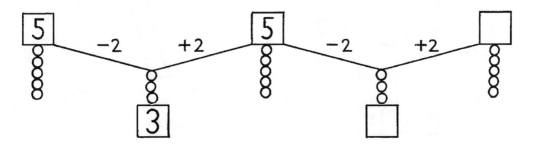

Count the peas in this pod and number them 1 to 7.

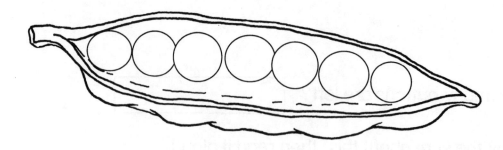

Here is part of a number line. You can use it to finish these sums.

5   6   7   8   9

1 more than 7 is

1 less than 7 is

2 more than 7 is

2 less than 7 is

7 and 2 make

7 and 1 make

7 take away 1 makes

7 take away 2 makes

Complete the 'story of seven'.

7 + ☐ = 7
6 + ☐ = 7
5 + ☐ = 7
4 + ☐ = 7
3 + ☐ = 7
2 + ☐ = 7
1 + ☐ = 7
0 + ☐ = 7

Colour.

Complete the number pairs to make 7.

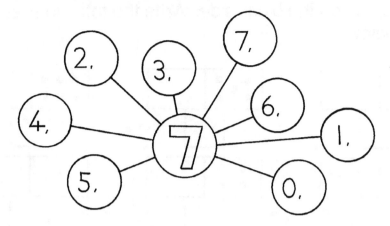

Finish the chain. Can you say it from memory?

Fill in the missing words.

Seven and [ ] make seven

Four less than seven is [ ]

Seven take away five is [ ]

Three and [ ] make seven

One and six make [ ]

[ ] and one make seven

Make each of these dominoes into a 'double' by drawing the same number of spots on the blank side. Write the total number of spots in the box below.

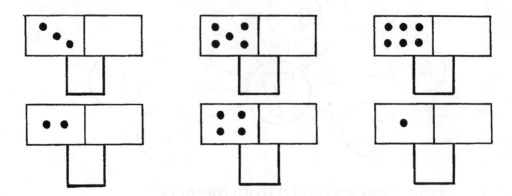

Double the number of sweets in each jar. How many now?

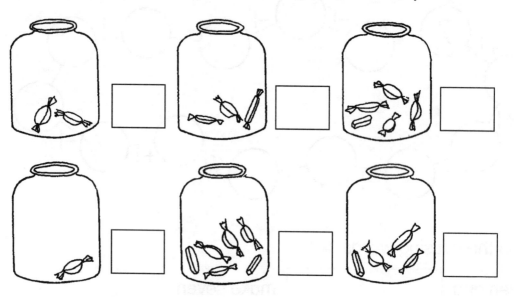

Read aloud then fill in the answer.

Double 5 is ☐   Double 1 is ☐

Double 3 is ☐   Double 4 is ☐

Double 6 is ☐   Double 2 is ☐

Colour one half of each circle black and the other yellow.

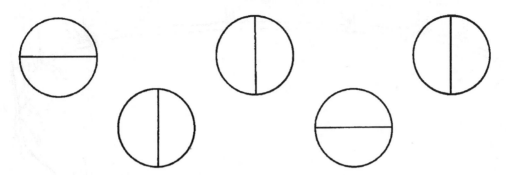

Give half the balloons to John and half to Pat.

Write the missing numbers.

Half of four is

Half of six is

Colour half the apple.

Half of ten is

Half of two is

Draw 8 ducks on the pond.

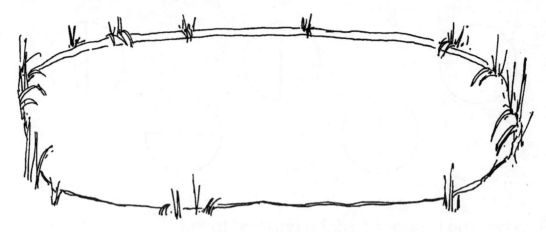

Complete the story of 8.

$0 +$ ⬚ $= 8$

$1 +$ ⬚ $= 8$

$2 +$ ⬚ $= 8$

$3 +$ ⬚ $= 8$

$4 +$ ⬚ $= 8$

$5 +$ ⬚ $= 8$

$6 +$ ⬚ $= 8$

$7 +$ ⬚ $= 8$

$8 +$ ⬚ $= 8$

Colour.

8

Start at 8 and finish the chain.

Complete the number pairs to make 8.

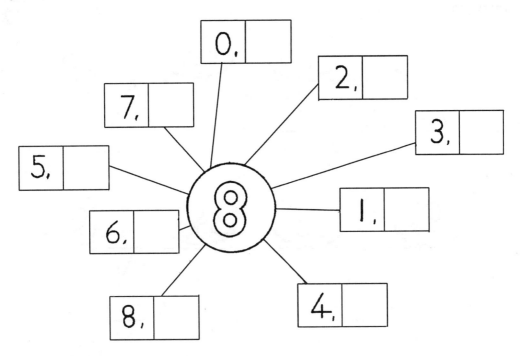

Fill in the missing words.

Six and [ ] make eight

Three less than eight is [ ]

Eight take away five is [ ]

Two and [ ] make eight

Double [ ] makes eight

Half of eight is [ ]

Copy the pattern.

789 ◇ 789 ◇ 789 ◇ 789

Make the scales balance. Draw the marbles first then write the numbers.

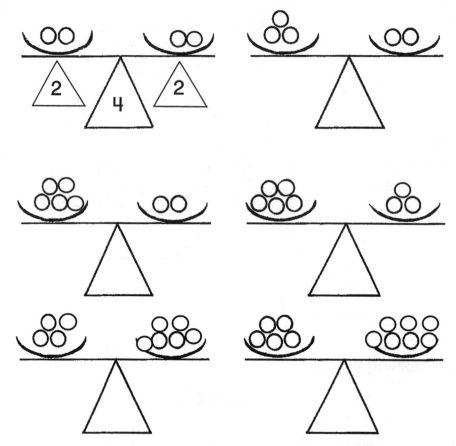

Eight children were playing in the park when ten more arrived. How many children were in the park then? Write your answer here.

Colour the picture.

Balance each side of the scale.

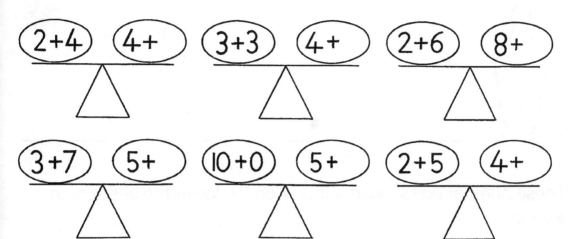

Write answers in words.

Four and two = three and [   ]

One less than ten = five and [   ]

Seven and one = four and [   ]

Six take away two = two and [   ]

Six and four = five and [   ]

Join with a pencil line the badges of the same value.
Colour the badges.

2+1   3+2   10−5

2+3   1+5   3+0

Draw nine skittles and number them from 1 to 9.

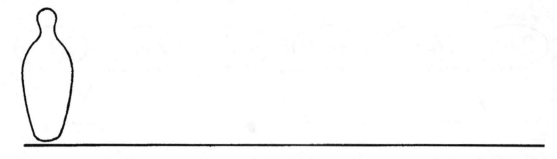

These number pairs make either 9 or 10. Write the answers in words.

6+3 →		1+8 →	
2+8 →		7+2 →	
5+5 →		3+7 →	
9+0 →		4+5 →	
1+9 →		3+6 →	

Finish all the sums about 9.

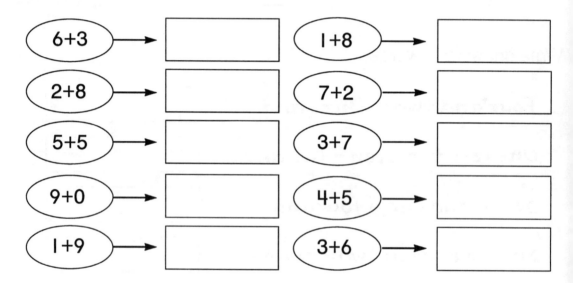

$9 + \boxed{} = 9$

$8 + \boxed{} = 9$

$7 + \boxed{} = 9$

$6 + \boxed{} = 9$

$5 + \boxed{} = 9$

$4 + \boxed{} = 9$

$3 + \boxed{} = 9$

$2 + \boxed{} = 9$

$1 + \boxed{} = 9$

$0 + \boxed{} = 9$

Fill in the missing words.

Eight and [   ] make nine

[   ] and five make nine

Three less than nine is [   ]

Nine take away four is [   ]

Two and [   ] make nine

[   ] and four make nine

Complete the pairs to make 9.

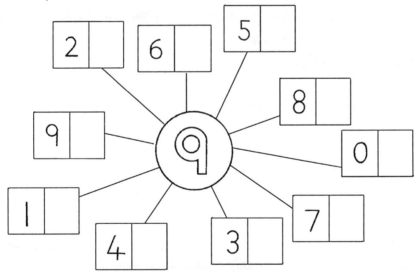

Copy the pattern.

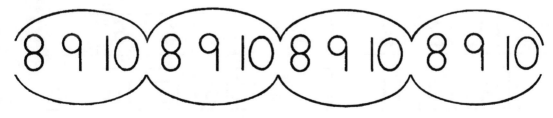

Count, then colour the doors. Choose a different colour for each door.

1st 2nd 3rd 4th 5th 6th 7th 8th 9th 10th

| 3 | 14 | 13 | 10 | 4 | 20 | 8 | 2 | 18 | 6 |

What number is on the 6th door? ☐

How many doors are there altogether? ☐

What colour is the 4th door? ☐

Which door shows the highest number? ☐

A story.
Sally coloured the first bear brown, the second bear black
    and the third bear yellow.
Make a picture like Sally.

Sally's picture

Write the fourth number.

11	12	13	
9	10	11	
18	19	20	

3	4	5	
16	17	18	
13	14	15	

Can you do these sums? Read them like this: 8 take away 2 equals 6.

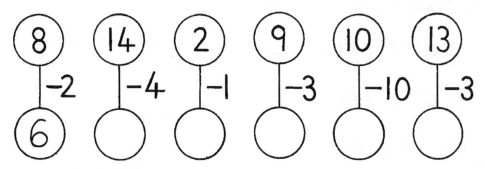

Join the labels which are equal.

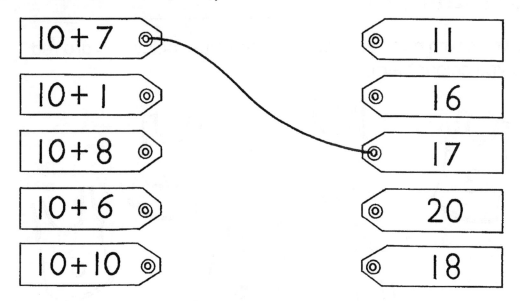

How many balloons altogether? Can you add the <u>totals</u> in each hand without counting in ones?

Can you do these sums? Write the answers in words.

Six and ten   = [   ]

Nine and ten   = [   ]

Four and ten   = [   ]

Eight and ten   = [   ]

One and ten   = [   ]

The vests with numbers above ten are blue, below ten are red. Can you colour them?

Fill in the missing numbers.

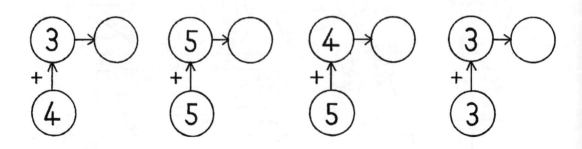

24

The sign > means 'is greater than', so 8>4 means 8 is greater than 4, and 6>5 means that 6 is greater than 5. The first two have been done for you. Can you do the rest?

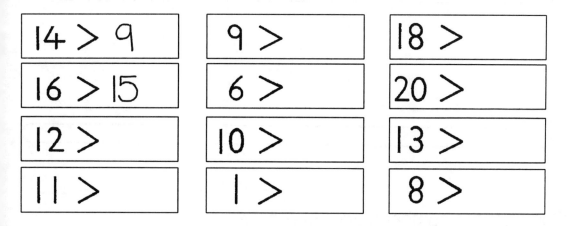

14 > 9	9 >	18 >
16 > 15	6 >	20 >
12 >	10 >	13 >
11 >	1 >	8 >

Colour the number cards which come between 8 and 16.

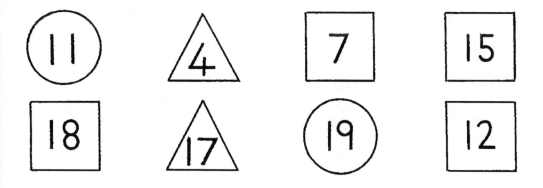

Write the number words then colour the labels which show even numbers.

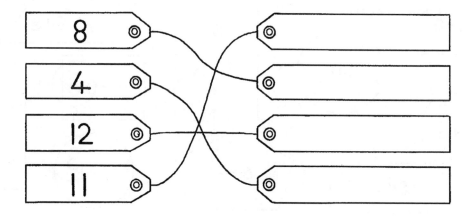

Draw ten rungs on the ladder.

Complete the number stories about ten.

10 + ☐ = 10
9 + ☐ = 10
8 + ☐ = 10
7 + ☐ = 10
6 + ☐ = 10
5 + ☐ = 10

4 + ☐ = 10
3 + ☐ = 10
2 + ☐ = 10
1 + ☐ = 10
0 + ☐ = 10

Colour the cards which make ten.

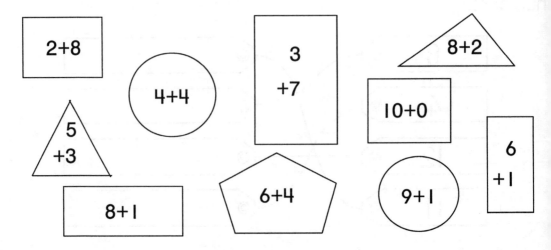

Write the missing words.

Six and [_____] make ten

Two and [_____] make ten

Three and [_____] make ten

Nine and [_____] make ten

Ten and [_____] make ten

Seven and [_____] make ten

Complete the number pairs to make ten.

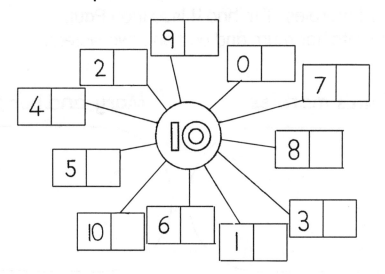

Fill in the missing numbers.

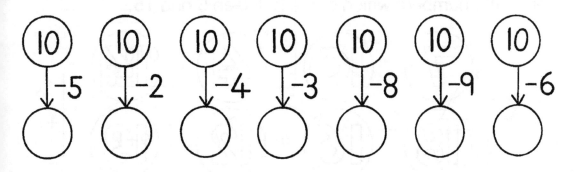

The sign < means 'is less than', so that 5<6 means 5 is less than 6, and 3<8 means 3 is less than 8. The first two have been done for you. Can you do the rest?

6 < 8	4 < 6	12 <
10 <	2 <	8 <
3 <	19 <	9 <
11 <	13 <	1 <

Two stories.
Paul had 14 marbles. Tim had 4 less than Paul.
Mary lived with her mum and dad and two sisters.
Draw

Tim's marbles   Mary and her family

Colour the numbers which come between 5 and 15.

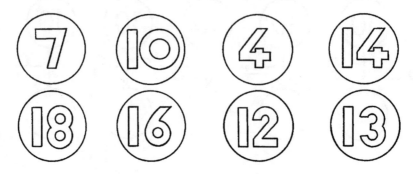

Nineteen or twenty?

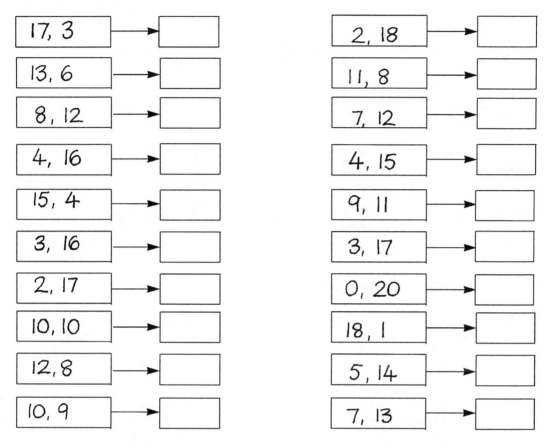

17, 3 → ☐	2, 18 → ☐
13, 6 → ☐	11, 8 → ☐
8, 12 → ☐	7, 12 → ☐
4, 16 → ☐	4, 15 → ☐
15, 4 → ☐	9, 11 → ☐
3, 16 → ☐	3, 17 → ☐
2, 17 → ☐	0, 20 → ☐
10, 10 → ☐	18, 1 → ☐
12, 8 → ☐	5, 14 → ☐
10, 9 → ☐	7, 13 → ☐

You are given 20p to buy
sweets. You spend 14p.
How much do you have left?

Start with the smallest amount and rearrange these coins in order
of value.

For this you will need either to use real money or to make cardboard coins.

Add 2.

$\longrightarrow$

8 $\longrightarrow$ 2 $\longrightarrow$ 3 $\longrightarrow$

18 $\longrightarrow$ 12 $\longrightarrow$ 13 $\longrightarrow$

28 $\longrightarrow$ 22 $\longrightarrow$ 23 $\longrightarrow$

38 $\longrightarrow$ 32 $\longrightarrow$ 33 $\longrightarrow$

What number comes before?

	14	15

	20	21

	27	28

	29	30

	19	20

	9	10

	38	39

	25	26

Write the numbers.

twenty one $\longrightarrow$ [ ]   thirty nine $\longrightarrow$ [ ]

twenty $\longrightarrow$ [ ]   forty $\longrightarrow$ [ ]

thirty $\longrightarrow$ [ ]   thirty five $\longrightarrow$ [ ]

thirty four $\longrightarrow$ [ ]   twenty six $\longrightarrow$ [ ]

Forty people were on a bus. Ten got off. How many people were left on the bus?

Can you give each child a total of 18p?

Start at 1 and colour every third tree, then number all the trees.

Complete the 100 square.

1	2	3	4	5	6	7	8	9	10
11	12	13	14	15	16	17	18	19	20
21	22	23	24	25			28		
			34	2		37			
				45	46				
				55	56				
			64		67				
		73					78		
	82							89	
91									100

Join the number to the word.

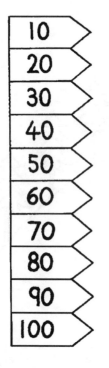

10
20
30
40
50
60
70
80
90
100

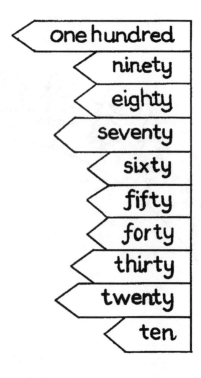

one hundred
ninety
eighty
seventy
sixty
fifty
forty
thirty
twenty
ten